INTRODUCTION

ART AND DRAWING HAS BEEN A PART OF MY LIFE
FROM THE MOMENT I STARTED DOODLING AS A KID.
THIS LOVE EVENTUALLY BECAME MY LIVING.
WHAT STARTED OFF AS CREATING A FEW TEE-SHIRT
DESIGNS FOR FRIENDS AND FAMILY QUICKLY BECAME
A FULL TIME BUSINESS AND MY BRAND NICKY ROCKETS
WAS SOON SELLING ALL OVER THE WORLD. LIFE WAS
WONDERFUL, CREATIVE, PROSPEROUS AND HEALTHY.
ALL THIS CHANGED IN 2015 I WOKE UP IN A HOSPITAL
BED AFTER SUFFERING A MASSIVE BRAIN HAEMORRHAGE.
RECOVERY TOOK NEARLY A YEAR.   THANKFULLY I ONLY
LOST USE OF MY LEFT ARM, AND I COULD STILL DRAW.
AS ALWAYS CREATIVITY WAS MY GATEWAY BACK TO HAPPINESS.
ALONG WITH THE MANY EXERCISES I WAS GIVEN BY MY
THERAPIST TO HELP REBUILD MY NOW
SLIGHTLY WONKY BODY AND INJURED BRAIN,
IT WAS DRAWING AND COLOURING
THAT REALLY HELPED ME
HEAL EMOTIONALLY.

HAPPY COLOURING

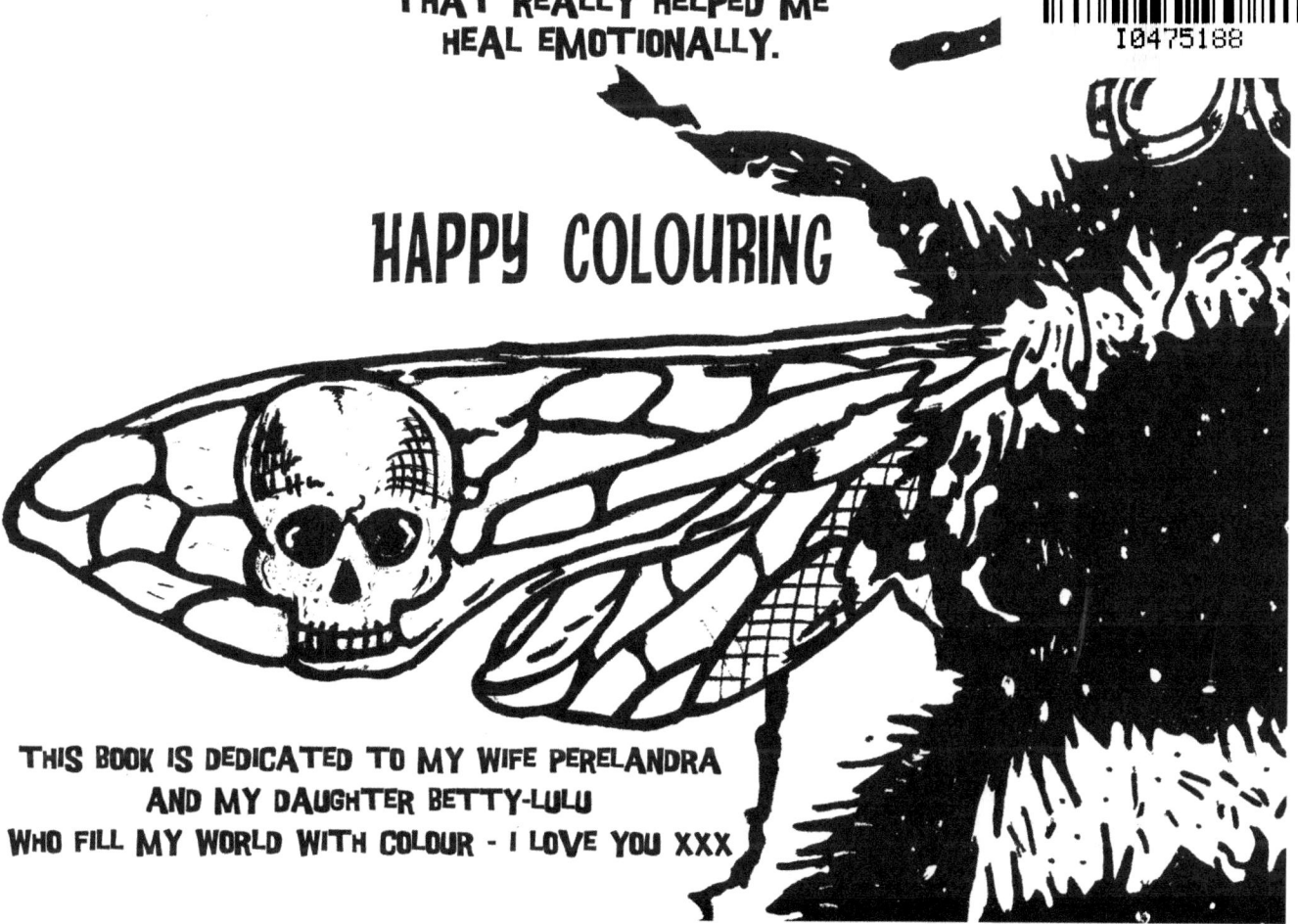

THIS BOOK IS DEDICATED TO MY WIFE PERELANDRA
AND MY DAUGHTER BETTY-LULU
WHO FILL MY WORLD WITH COLOUR - I LOVE YOU XXX

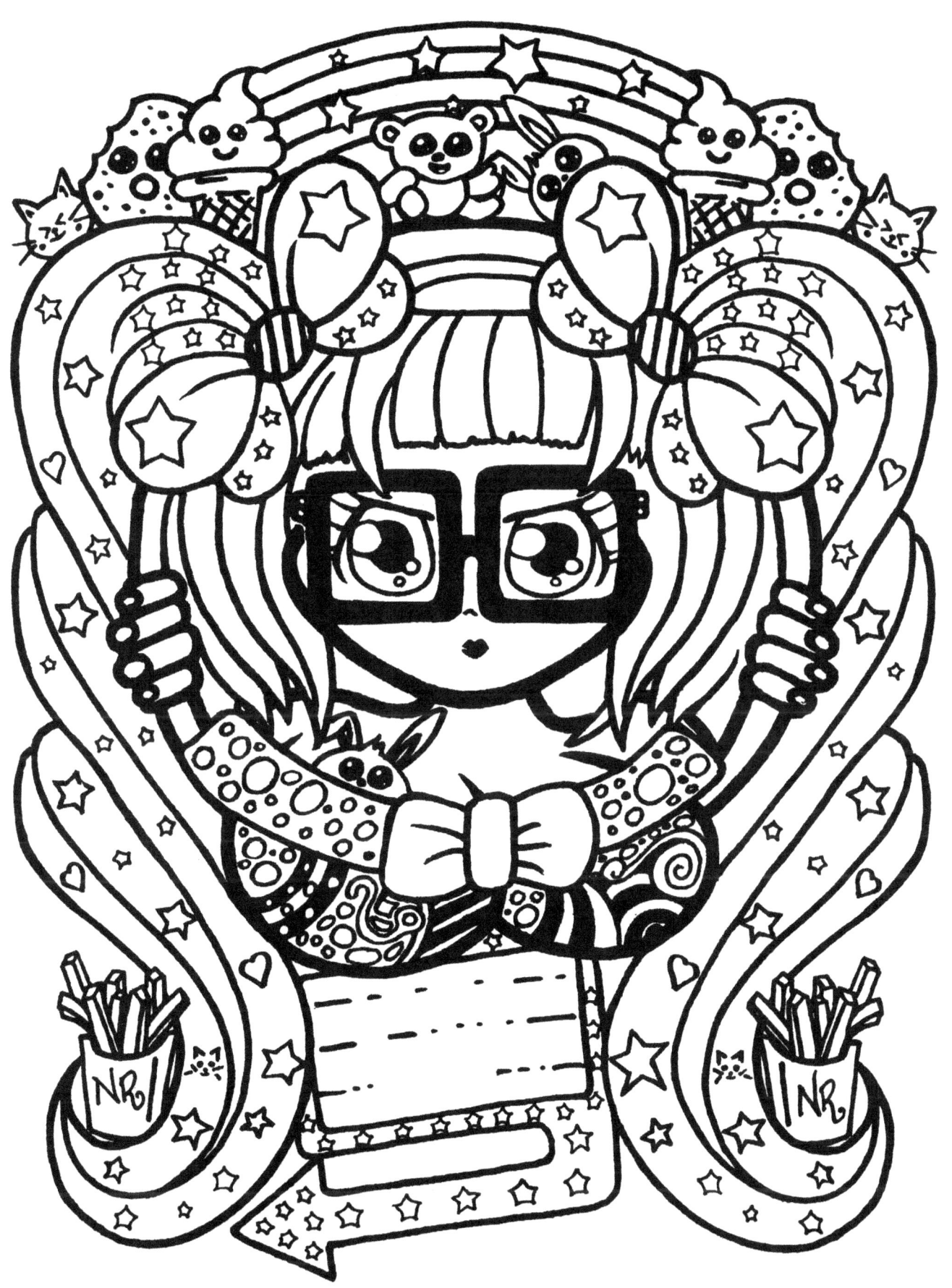

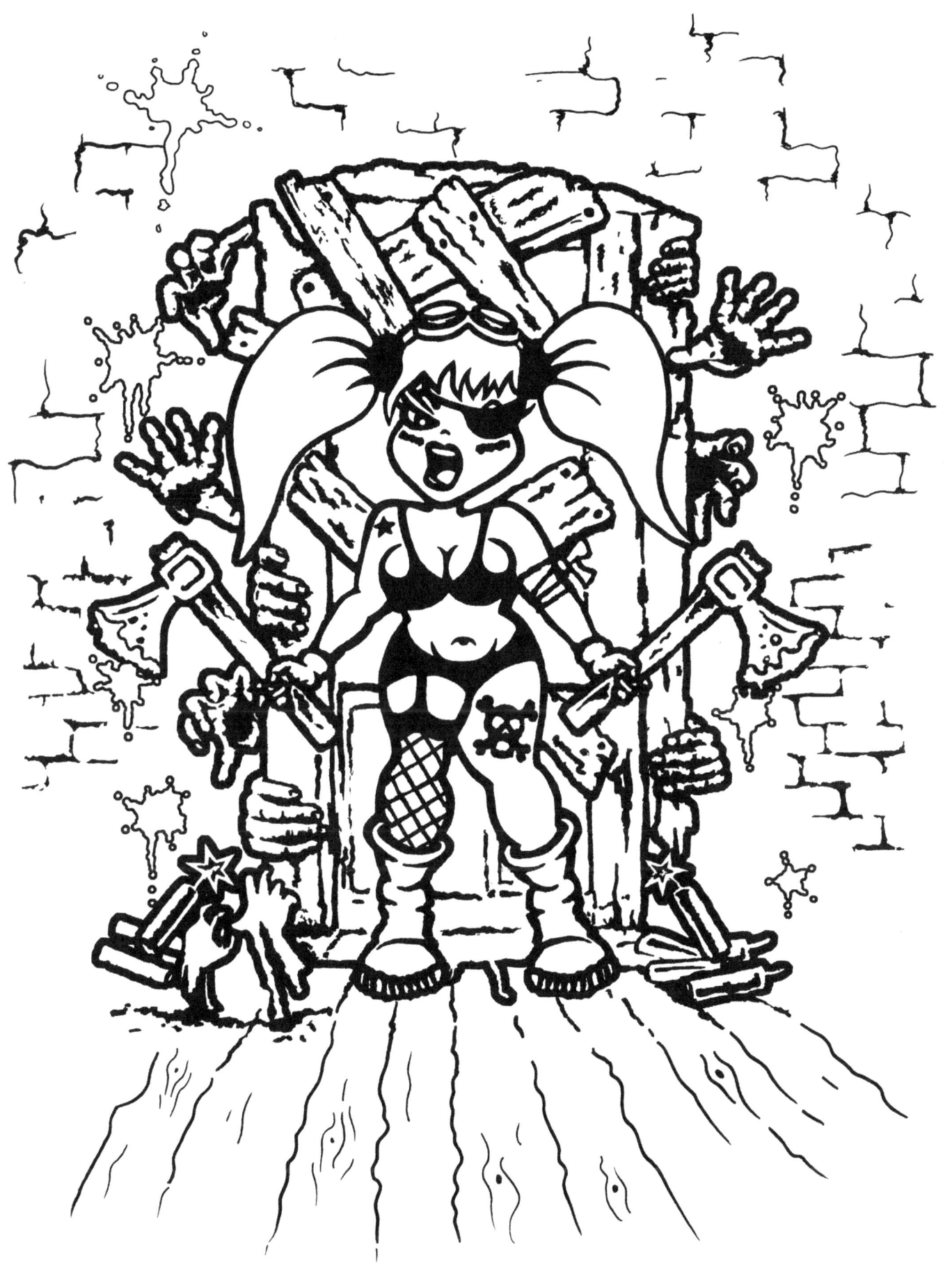

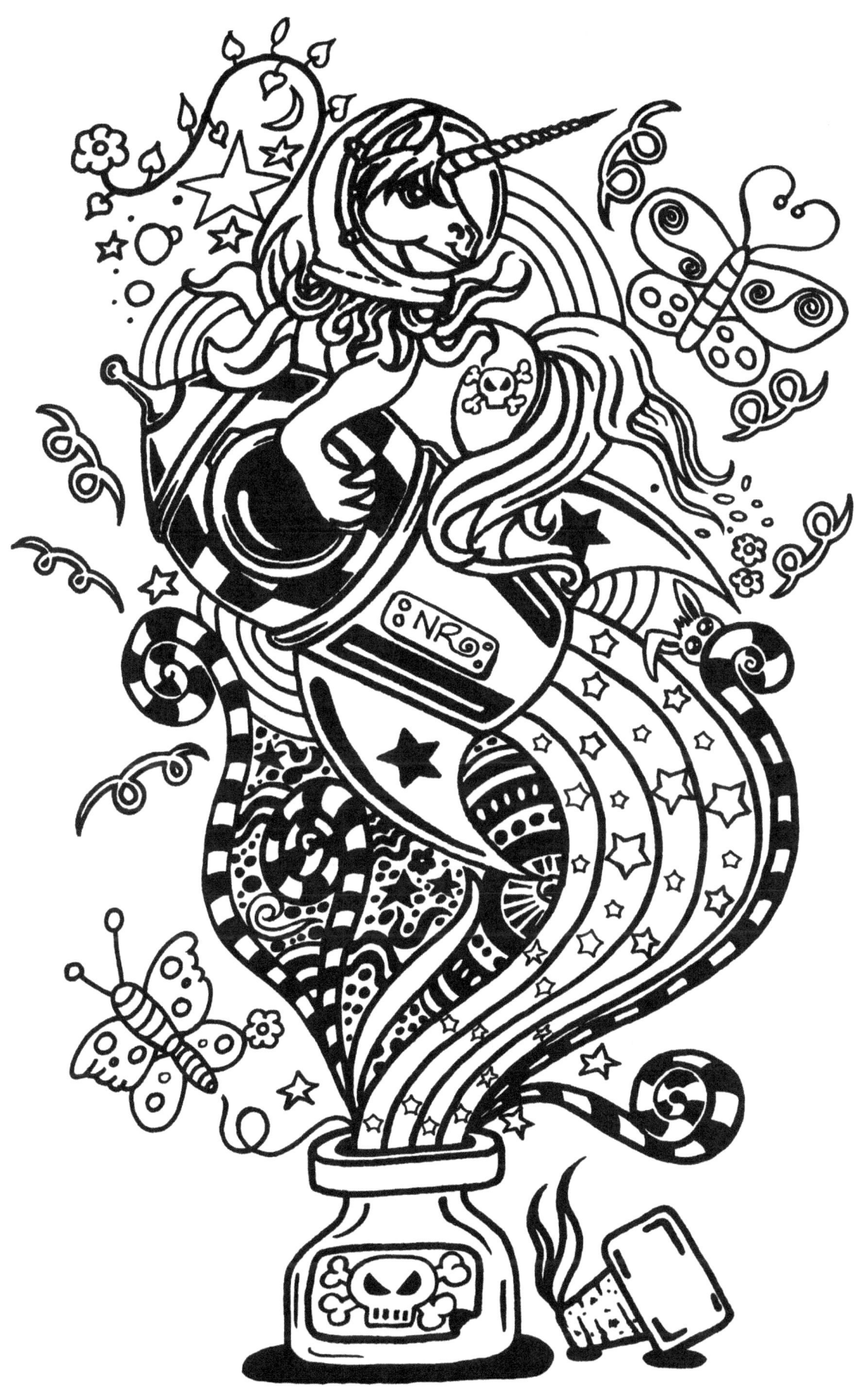

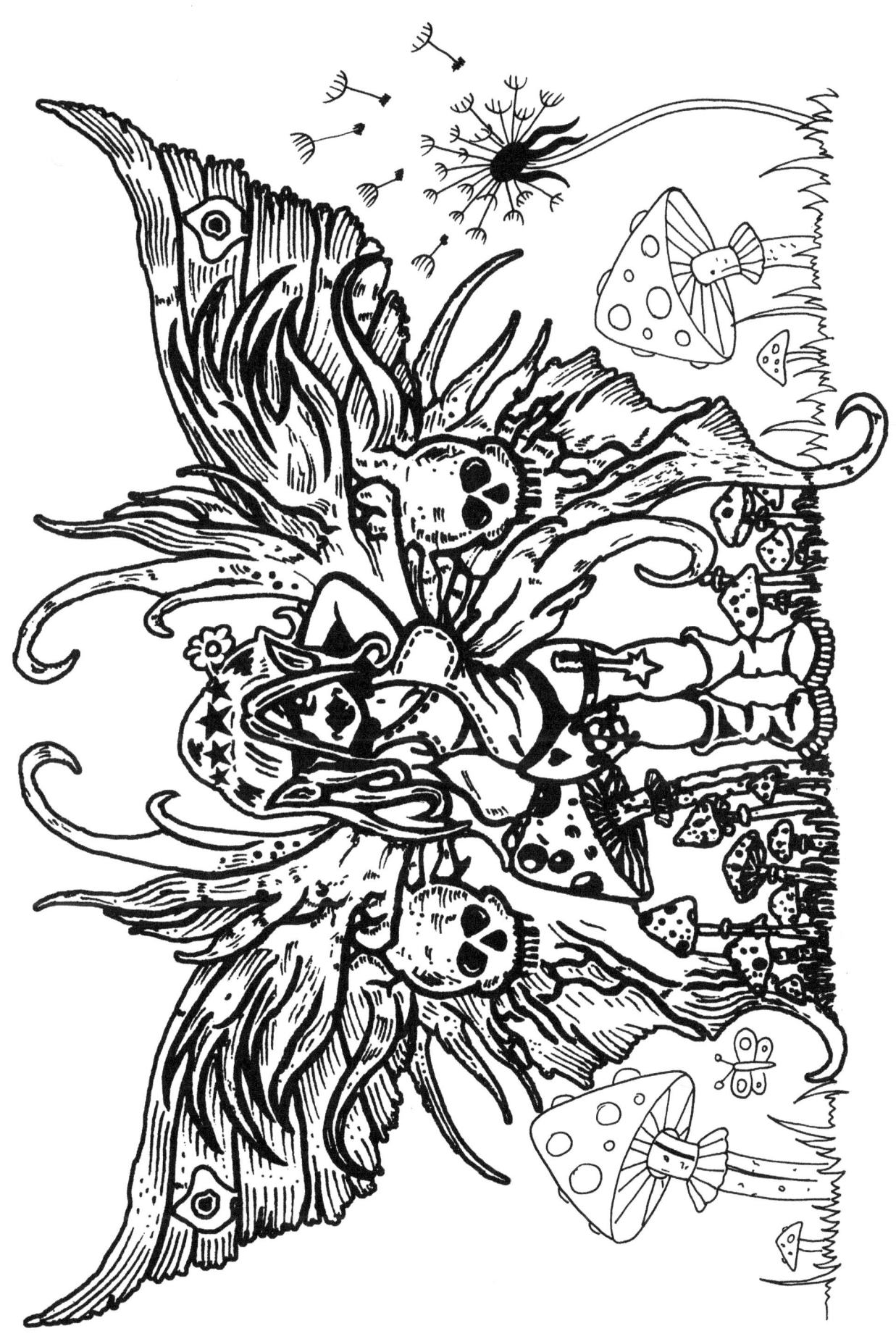

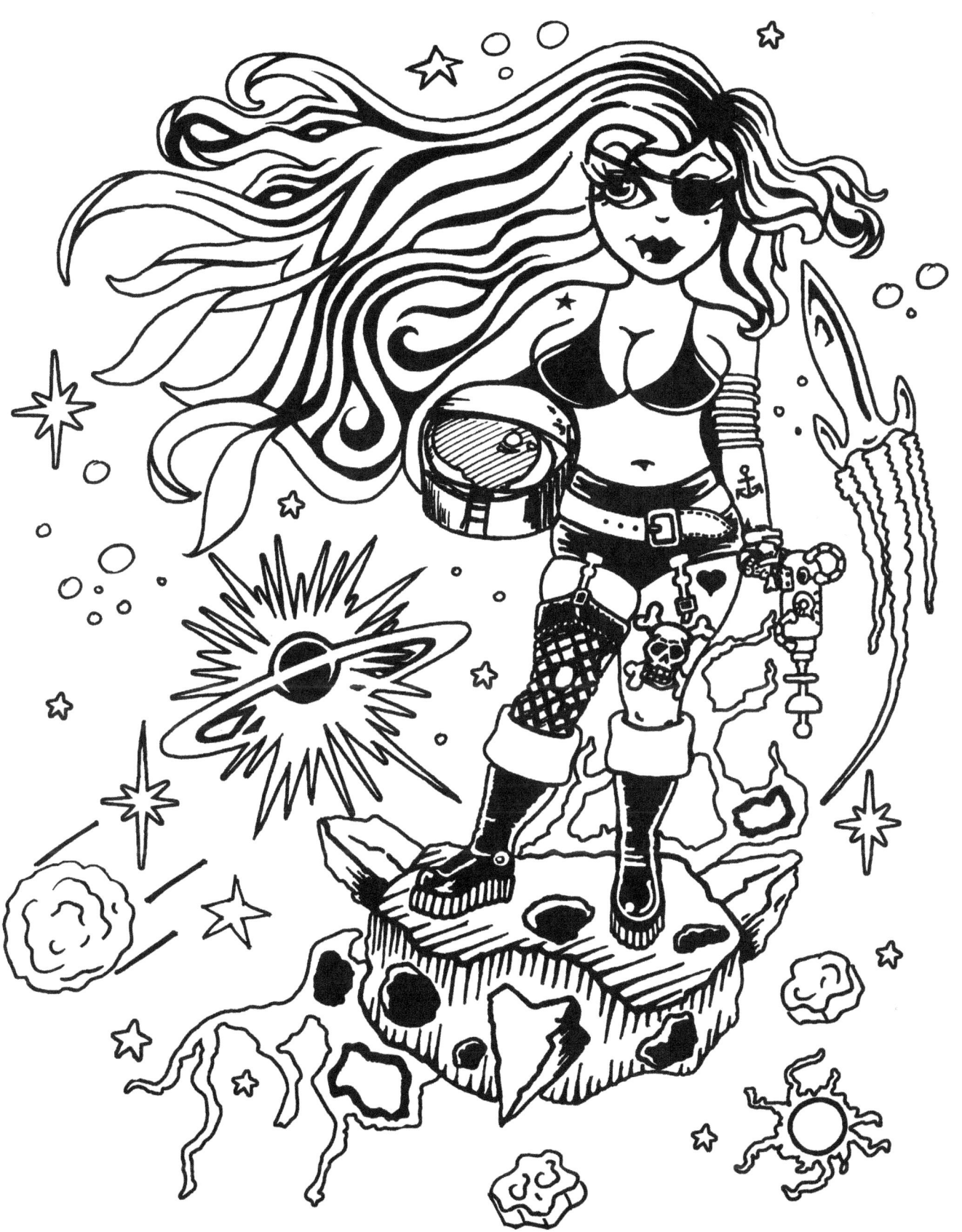

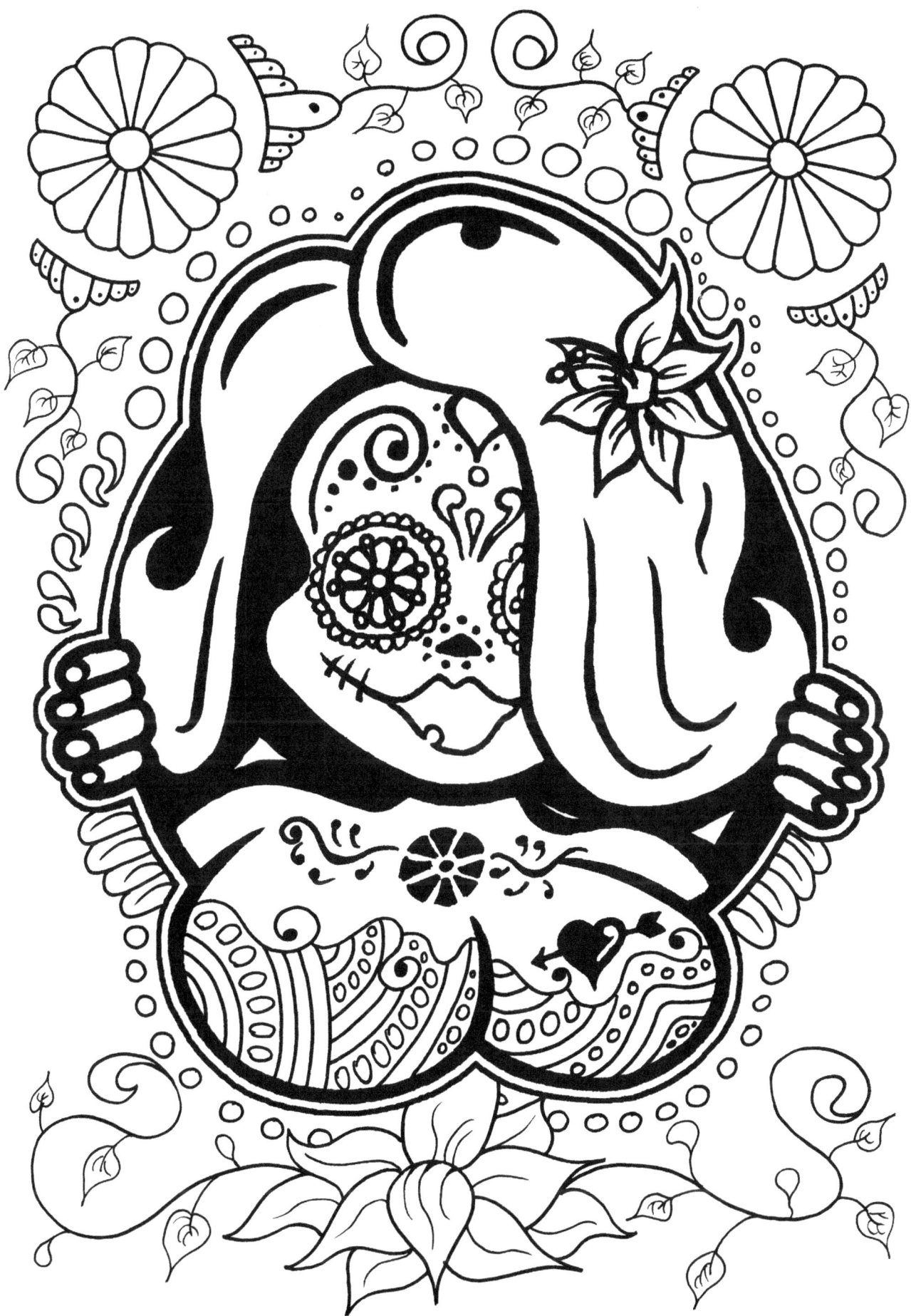

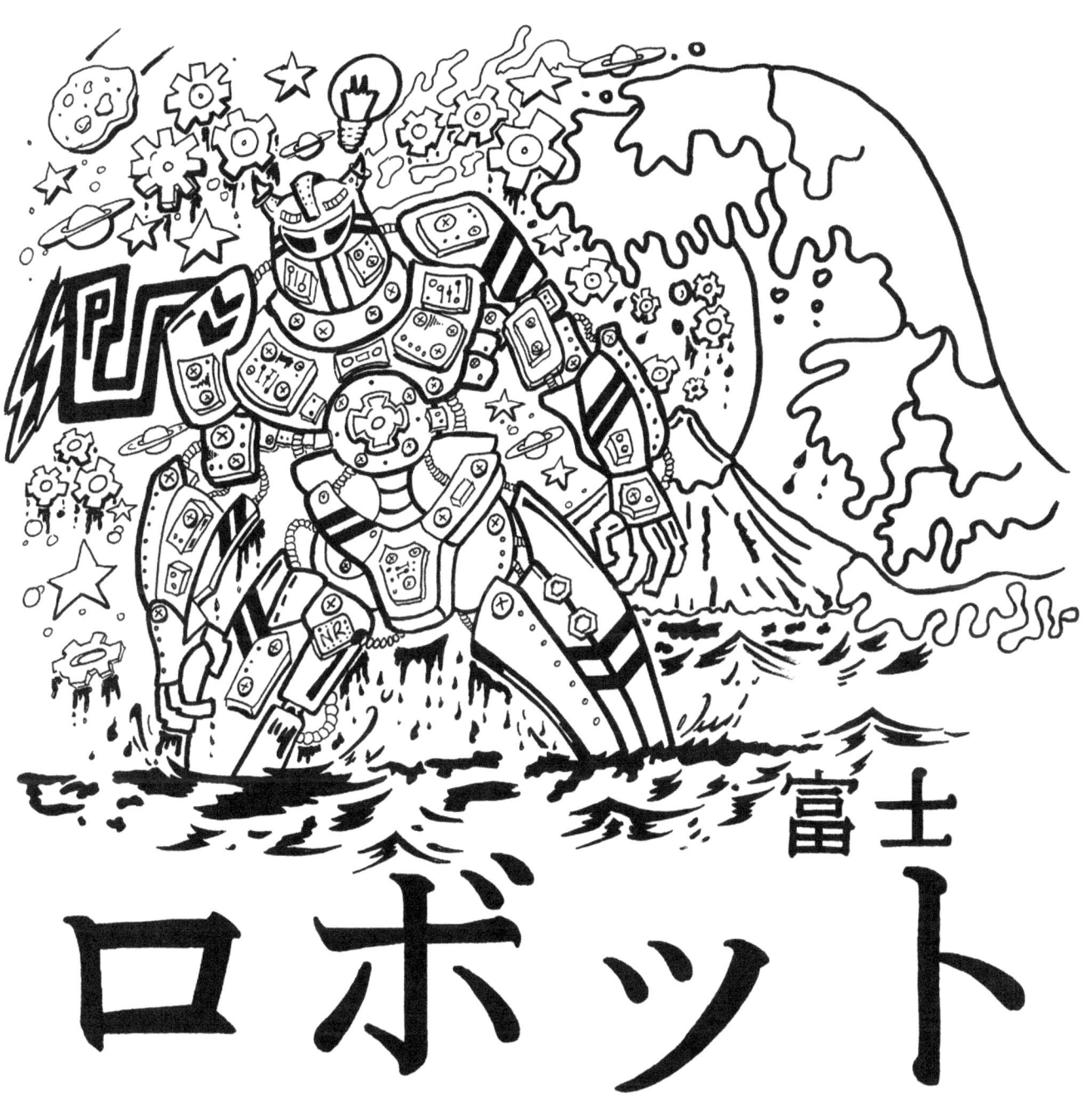

富士
ロボット

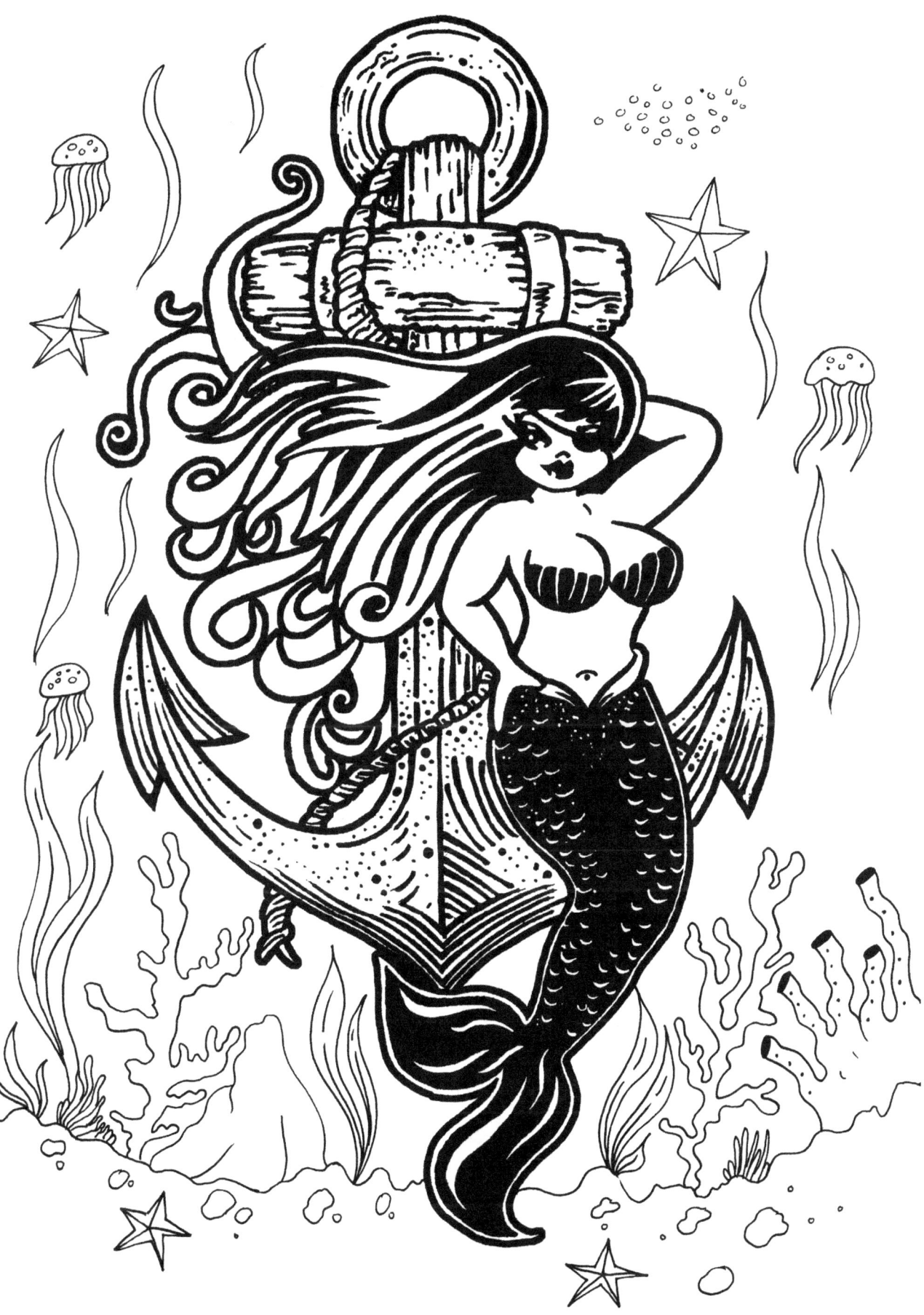

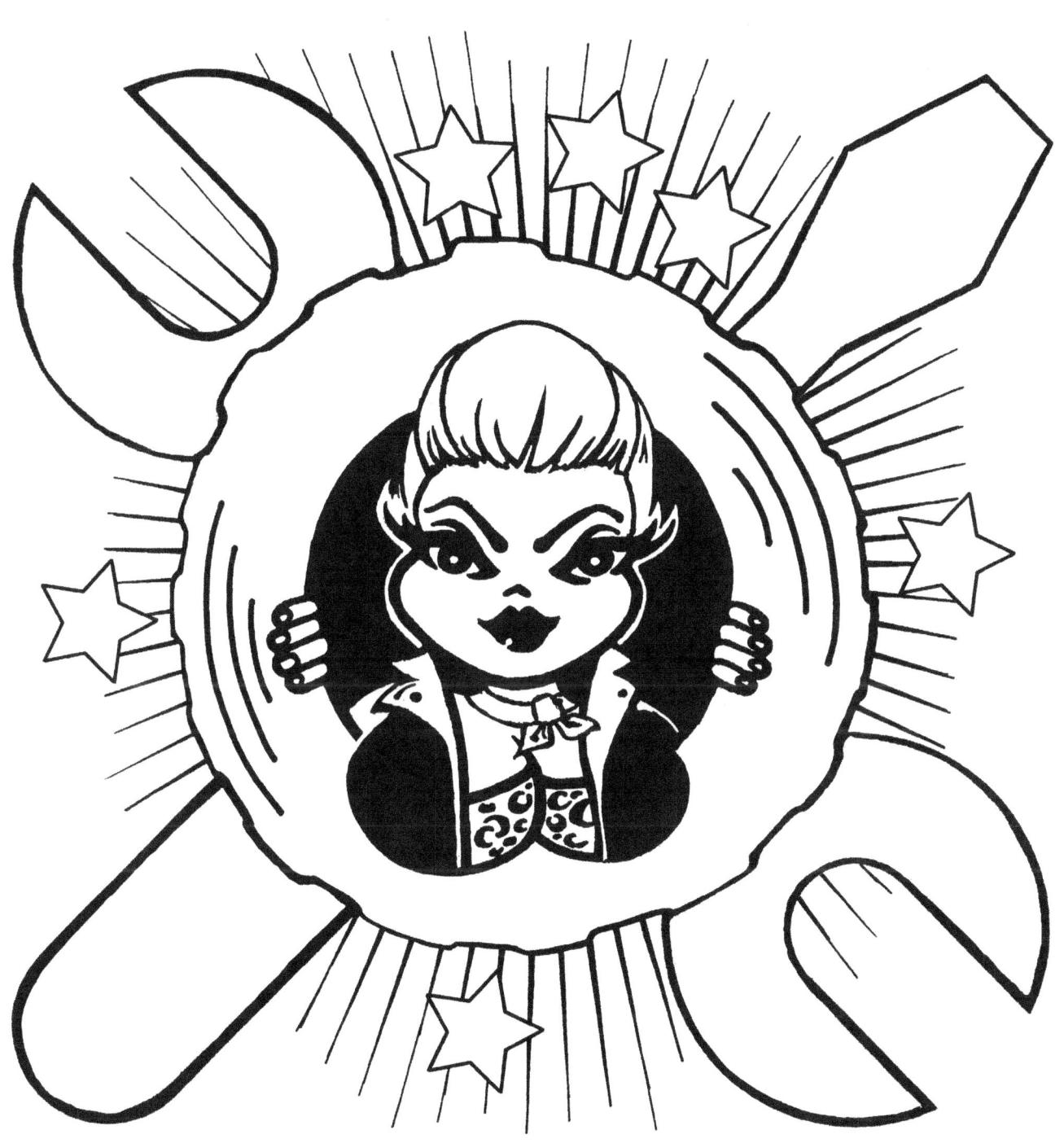

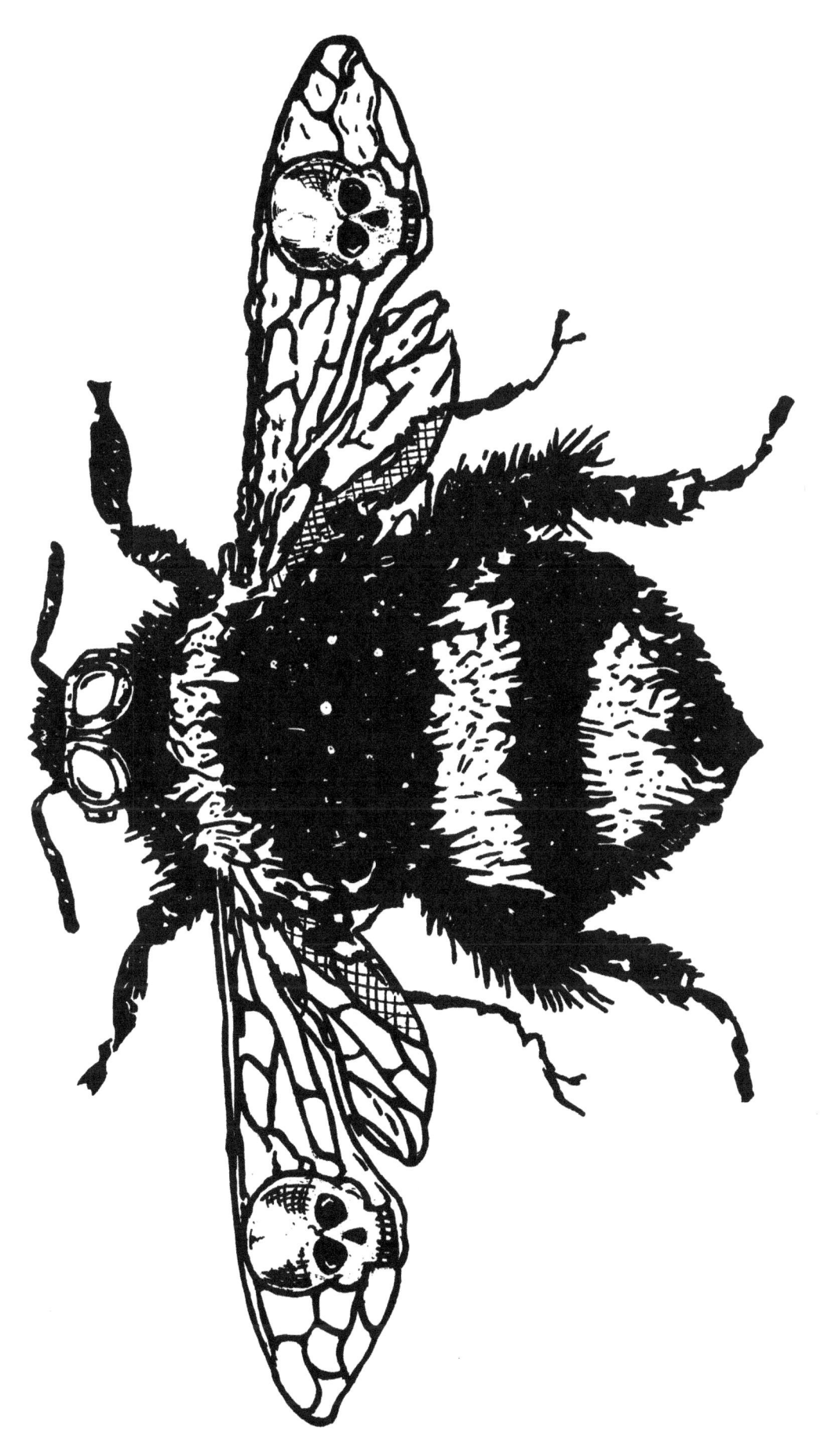

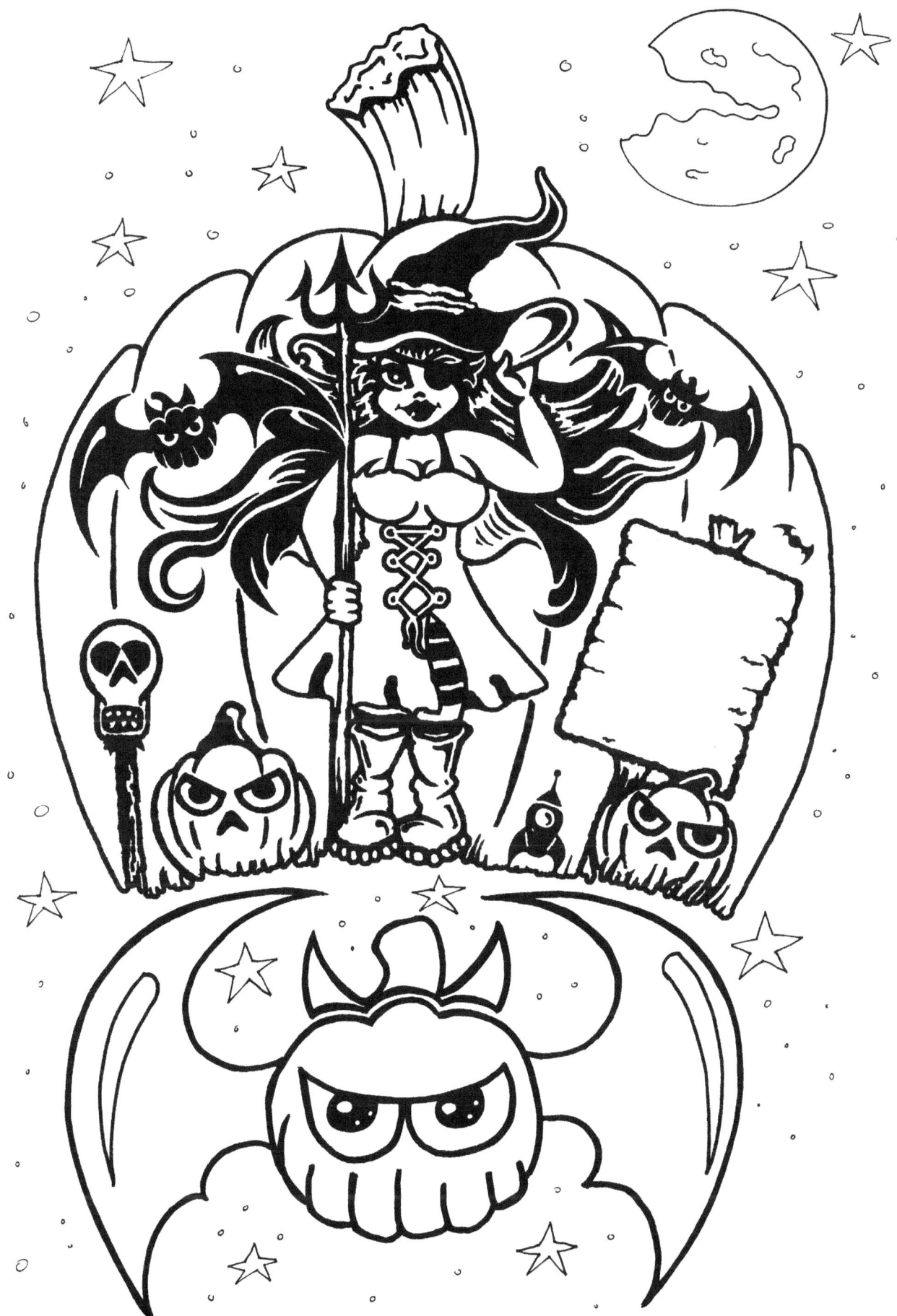

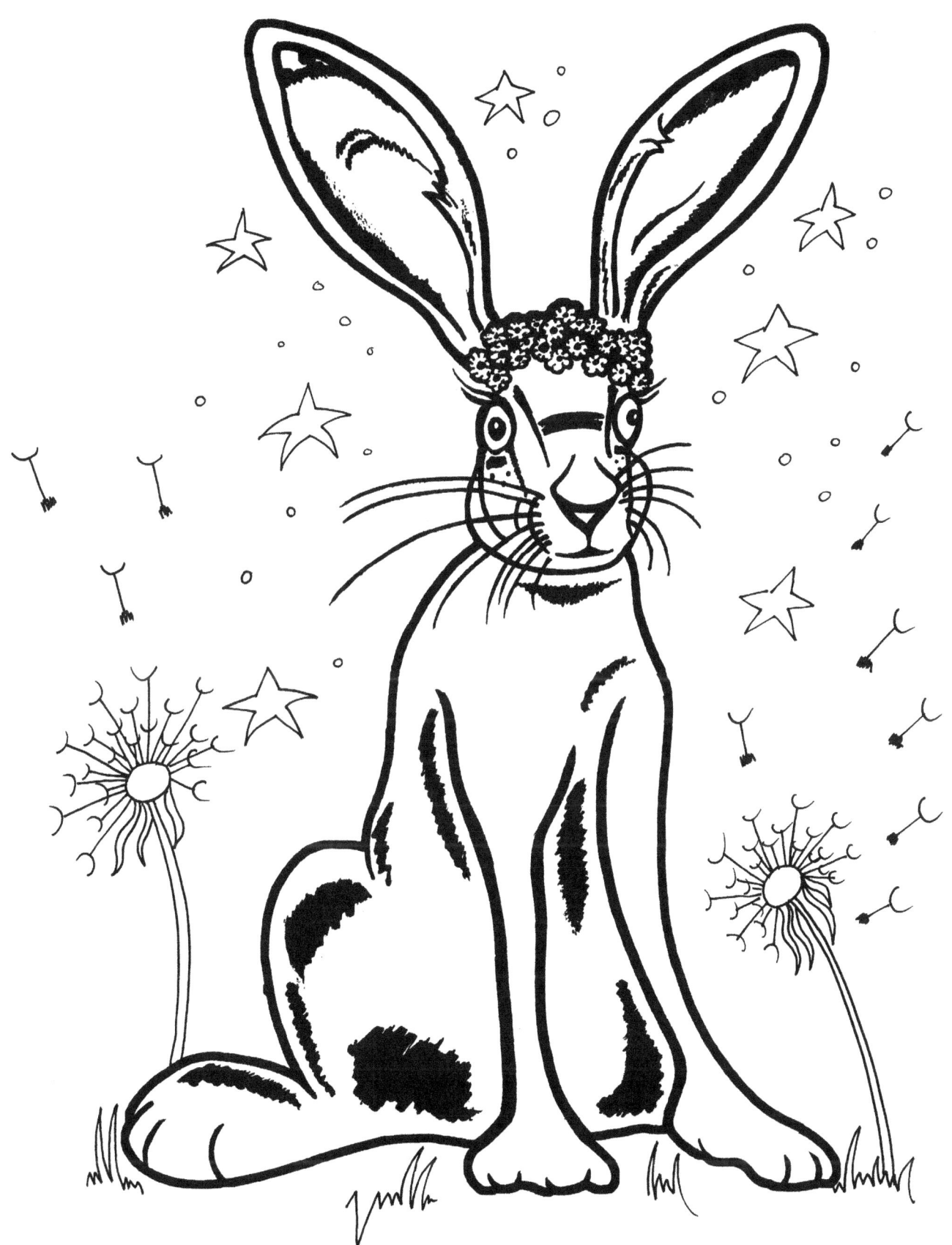

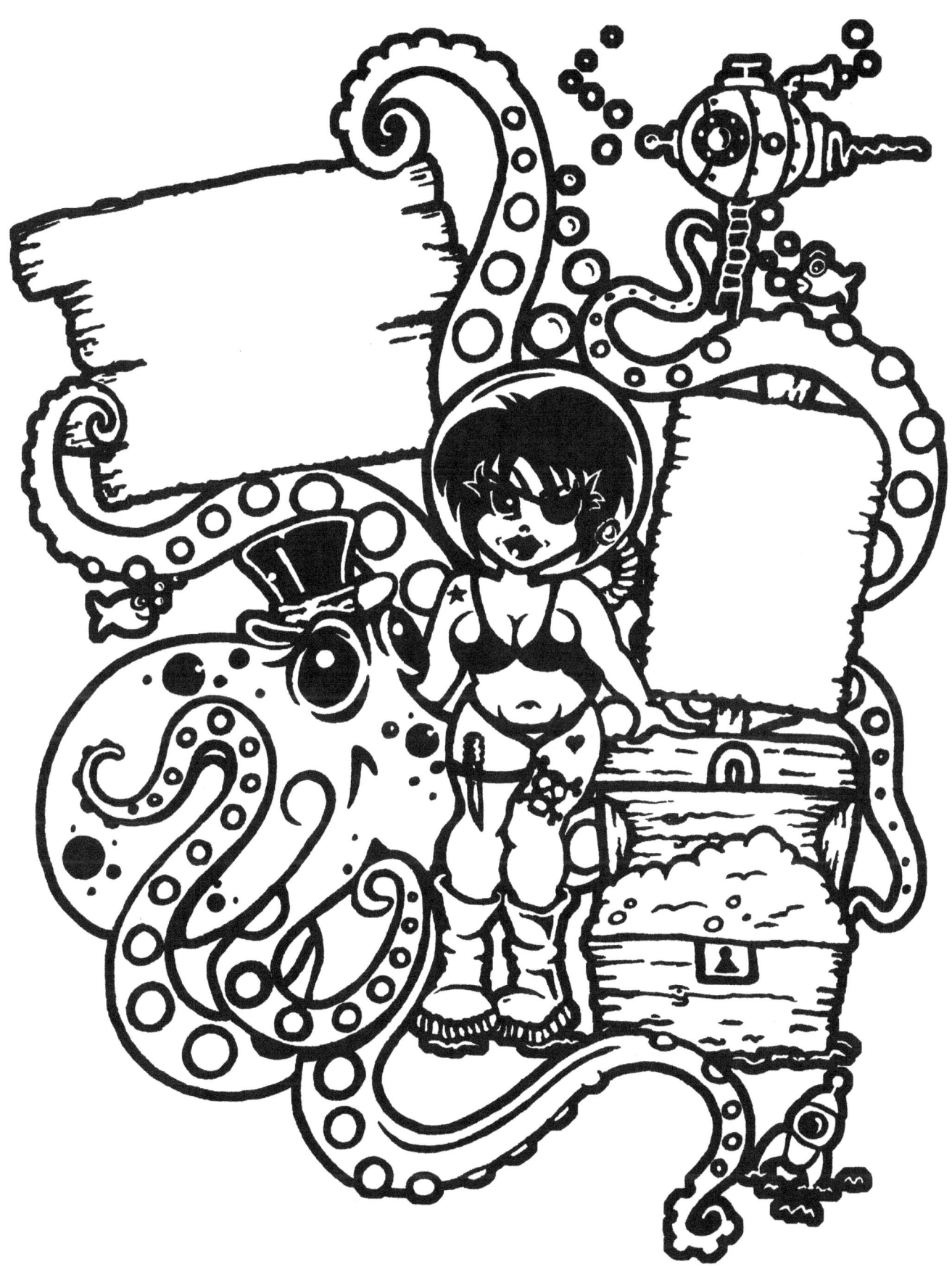

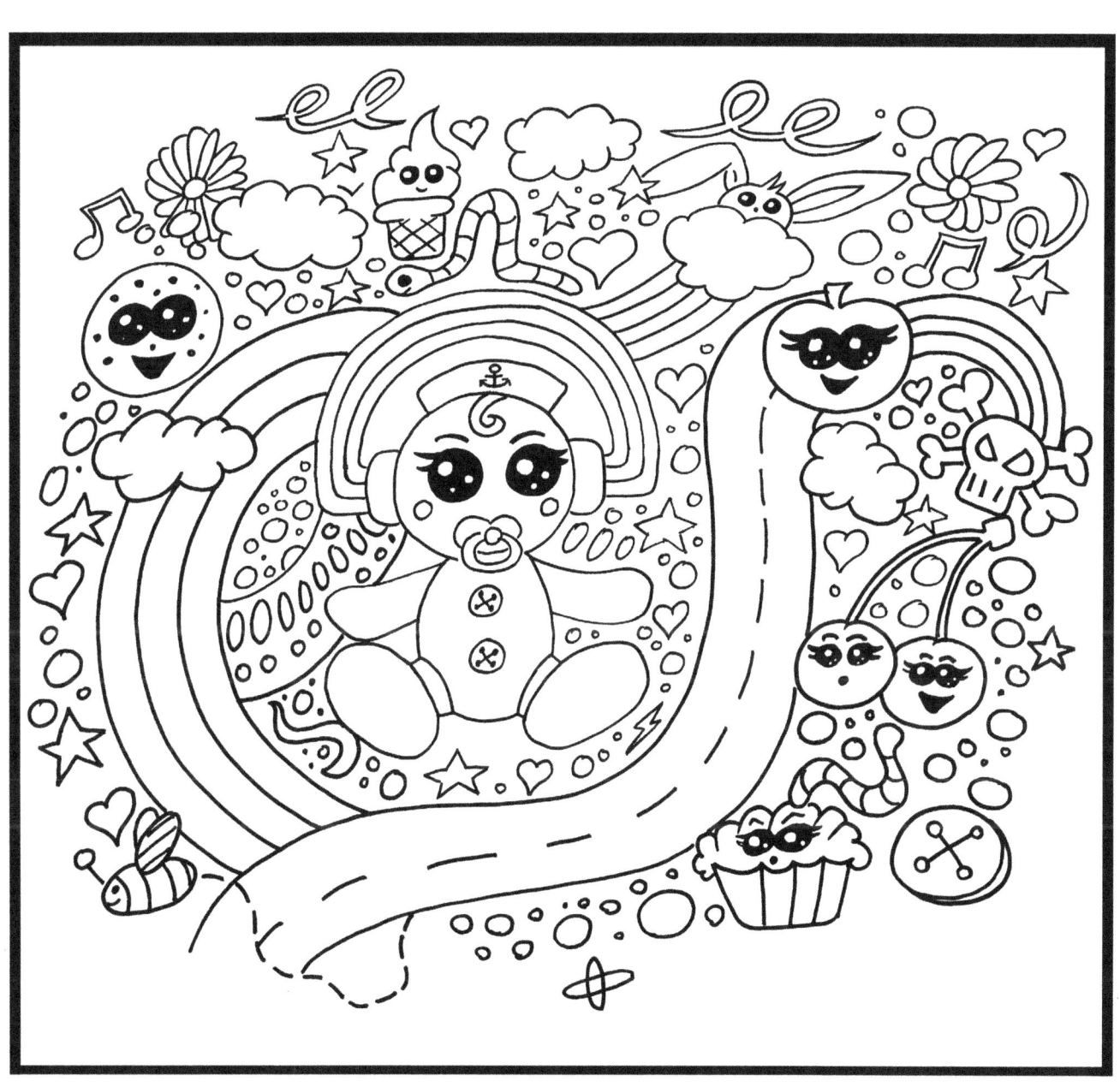

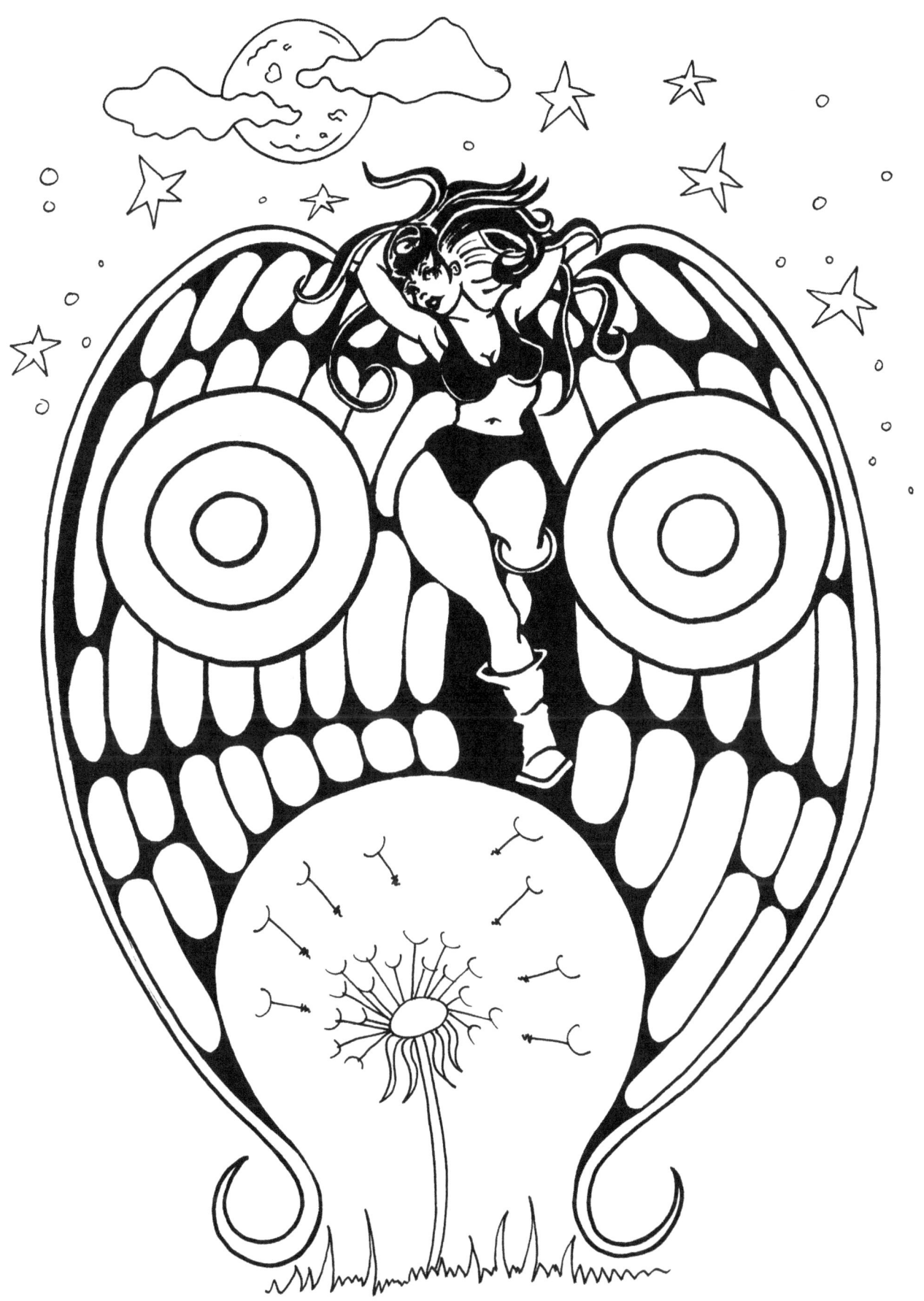

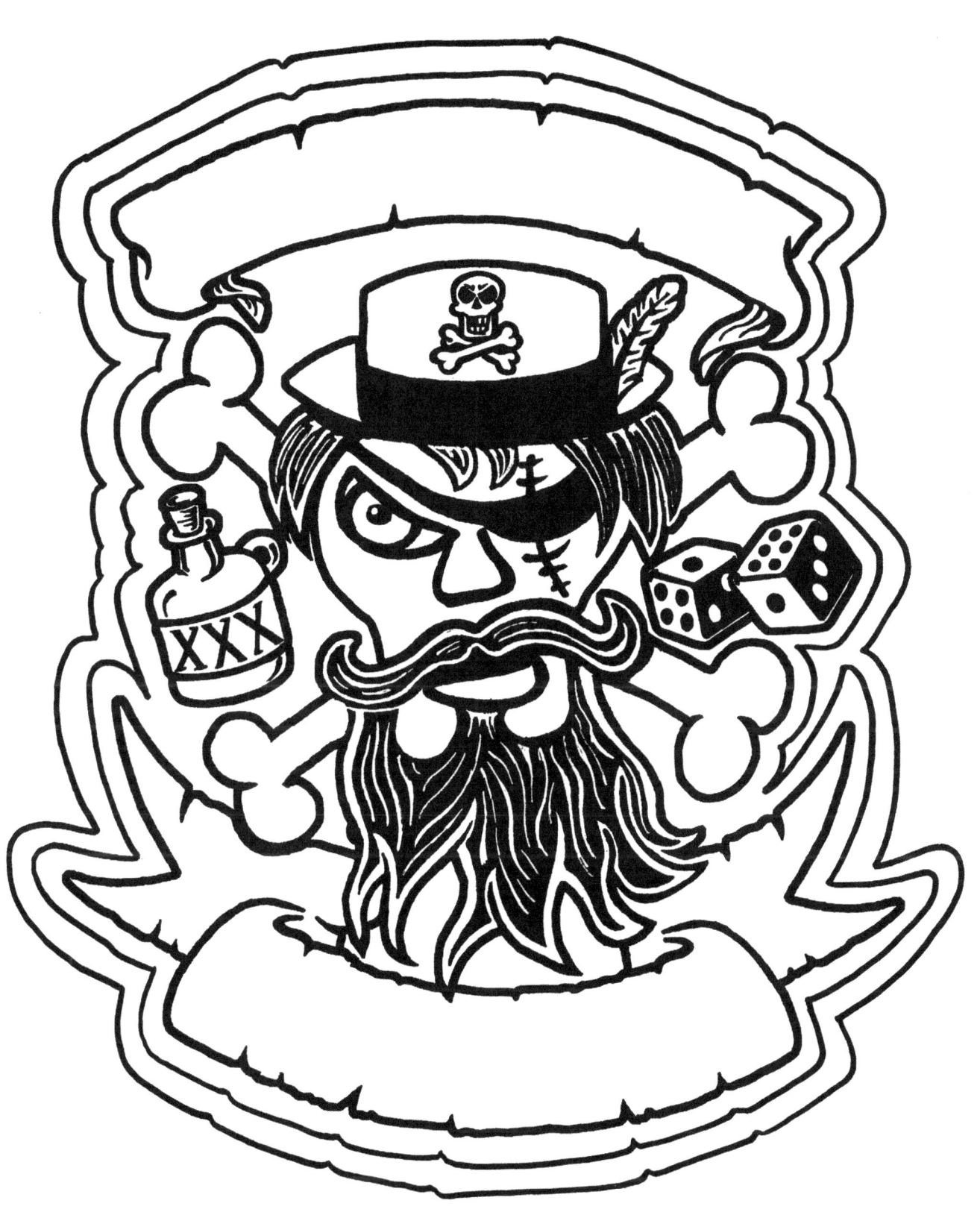

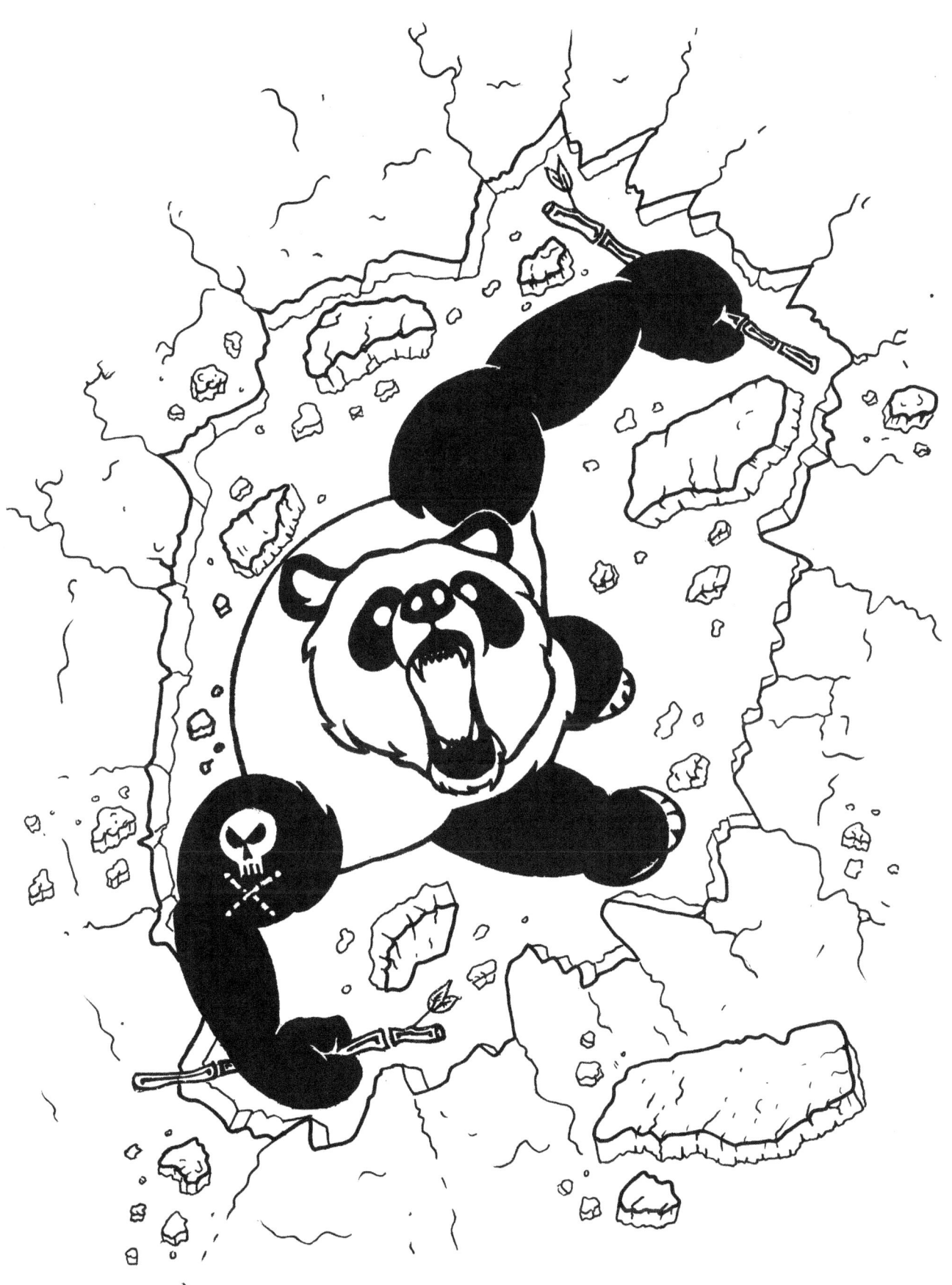

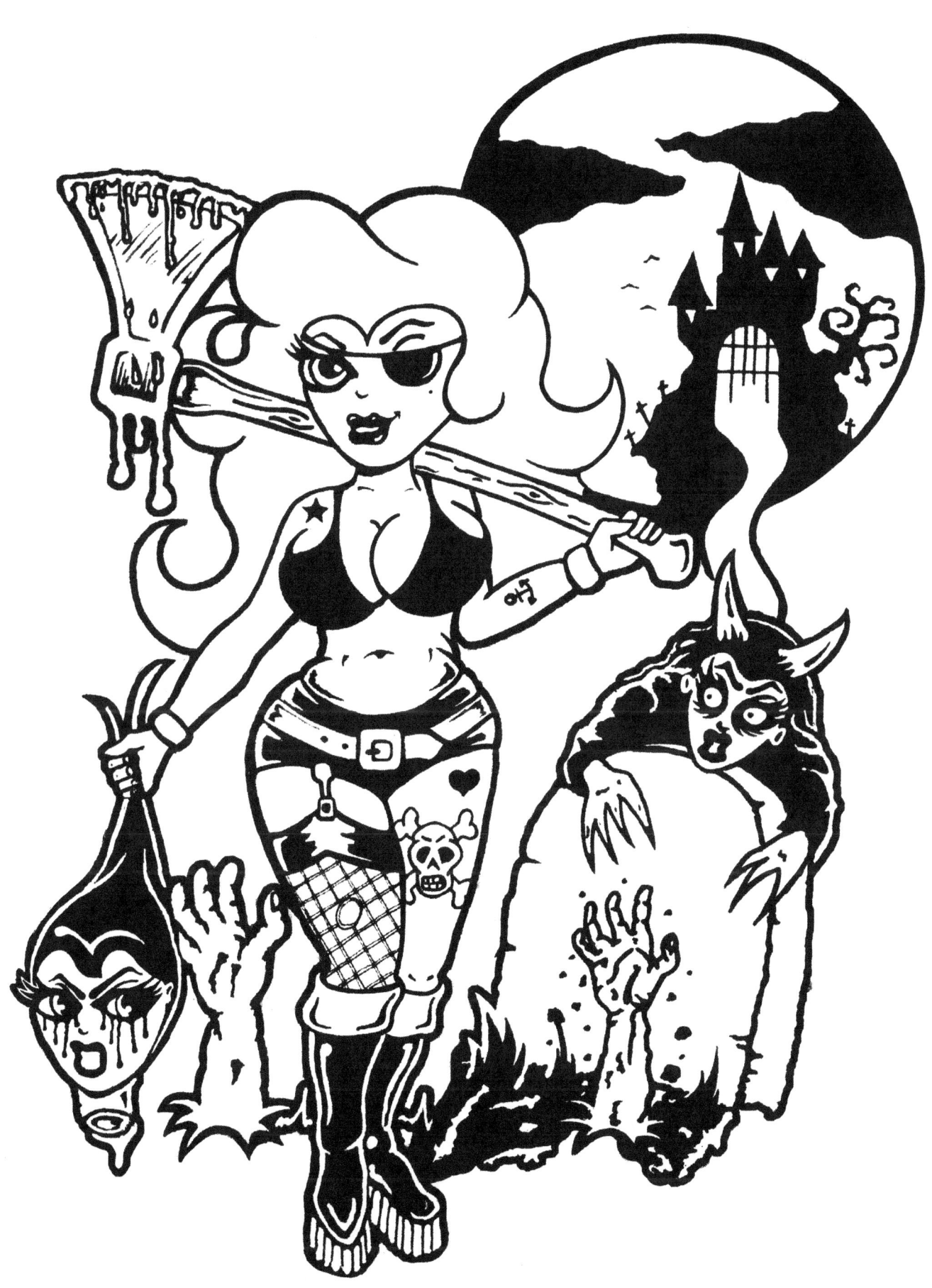

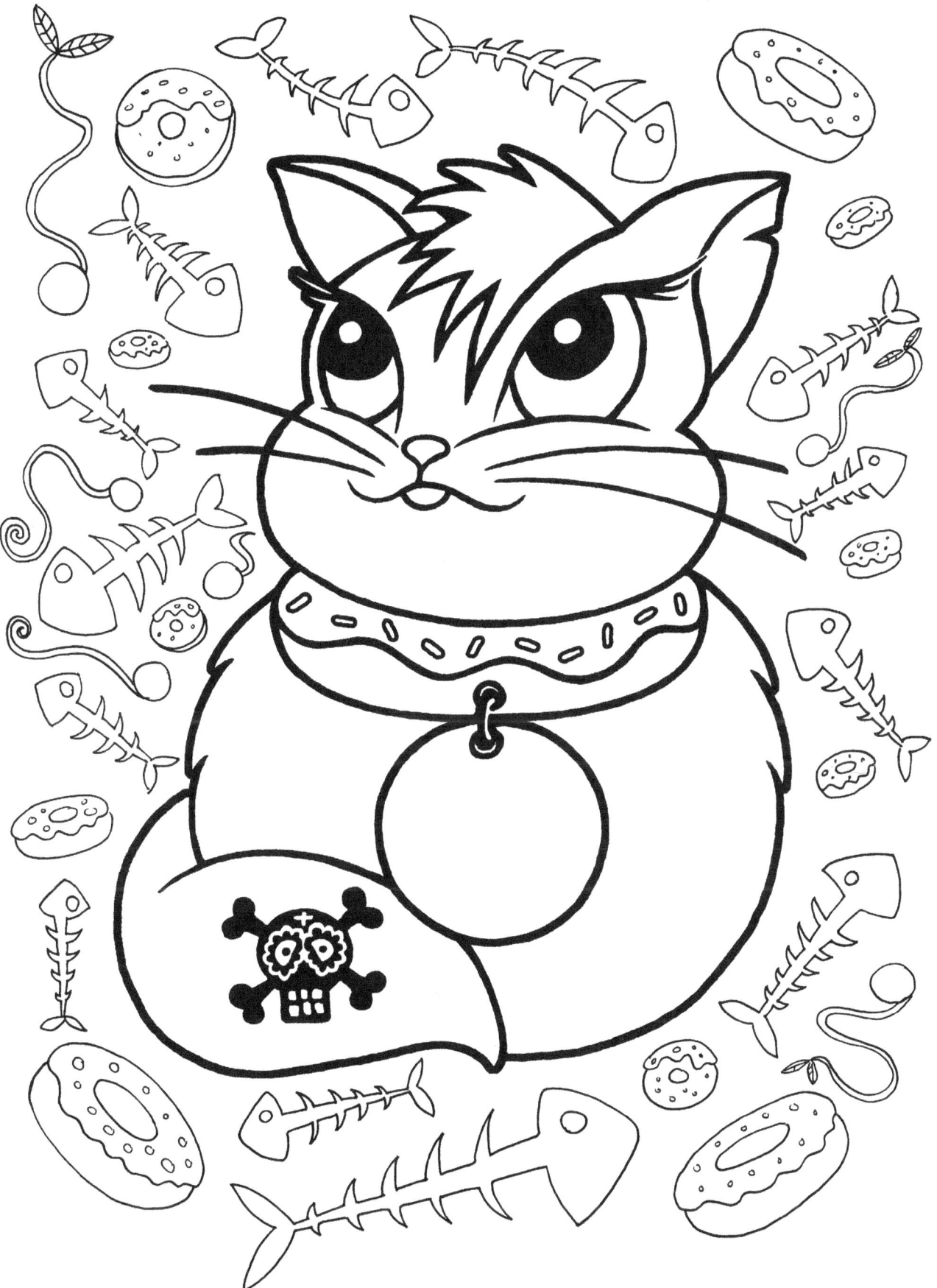

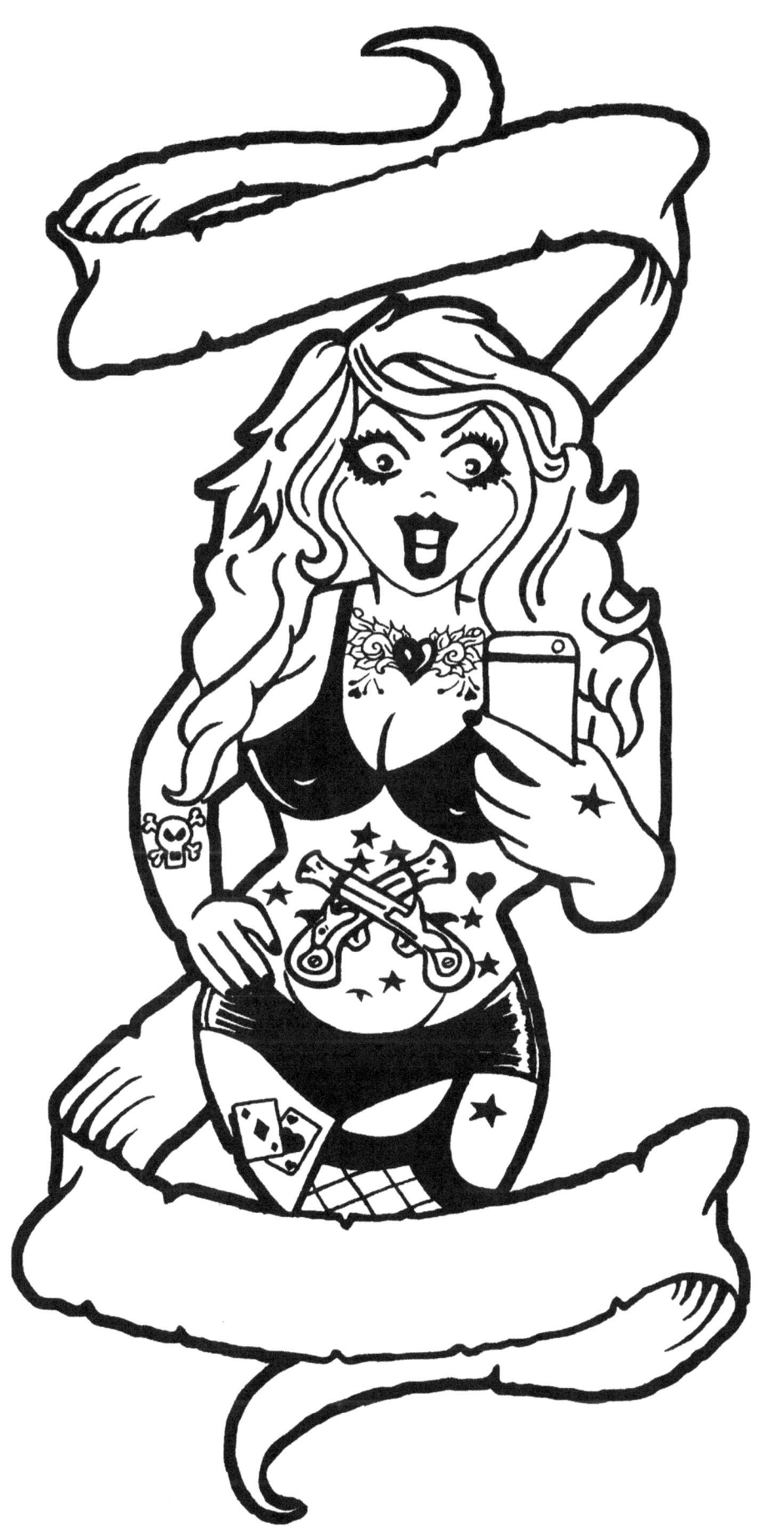

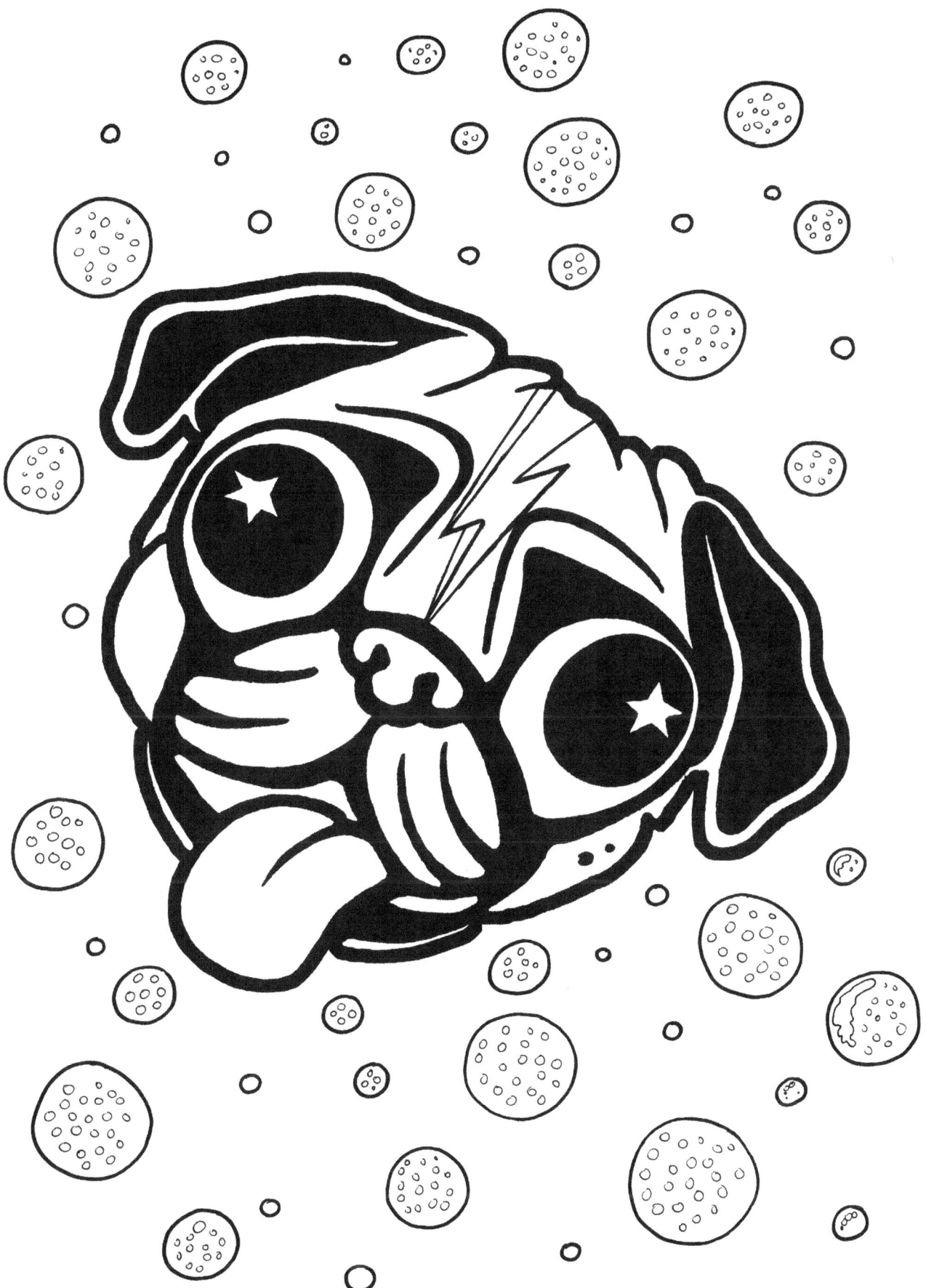

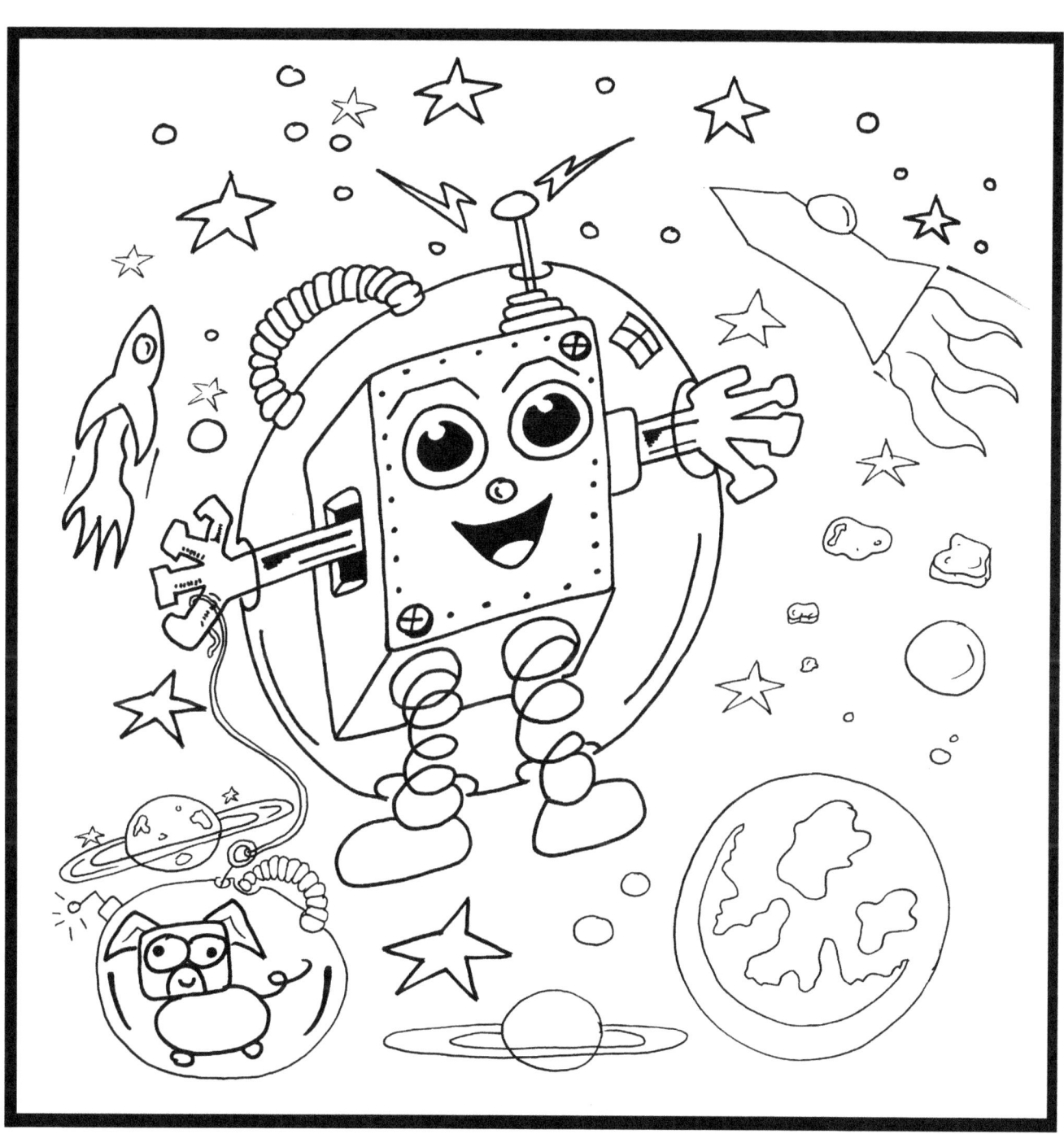

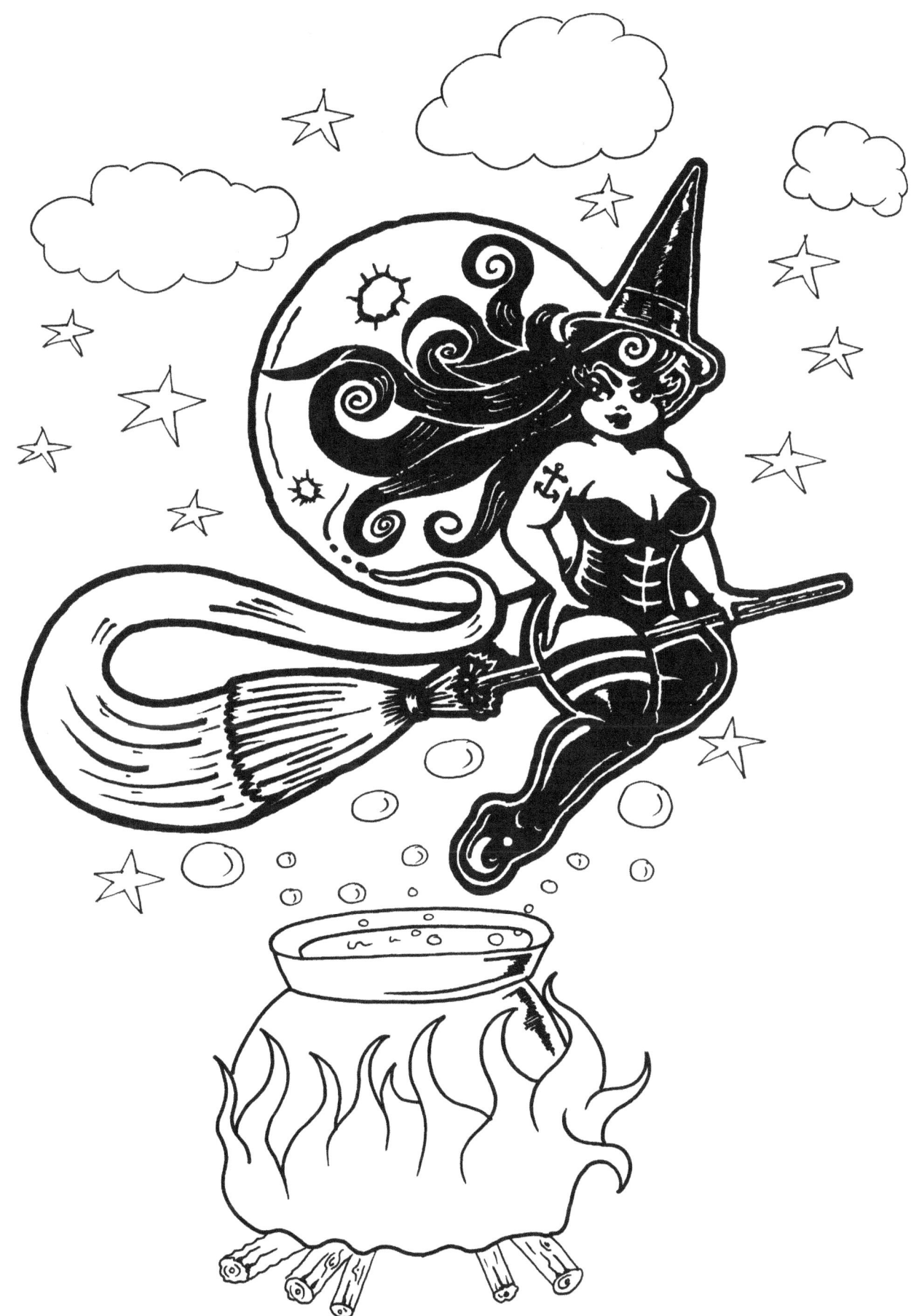

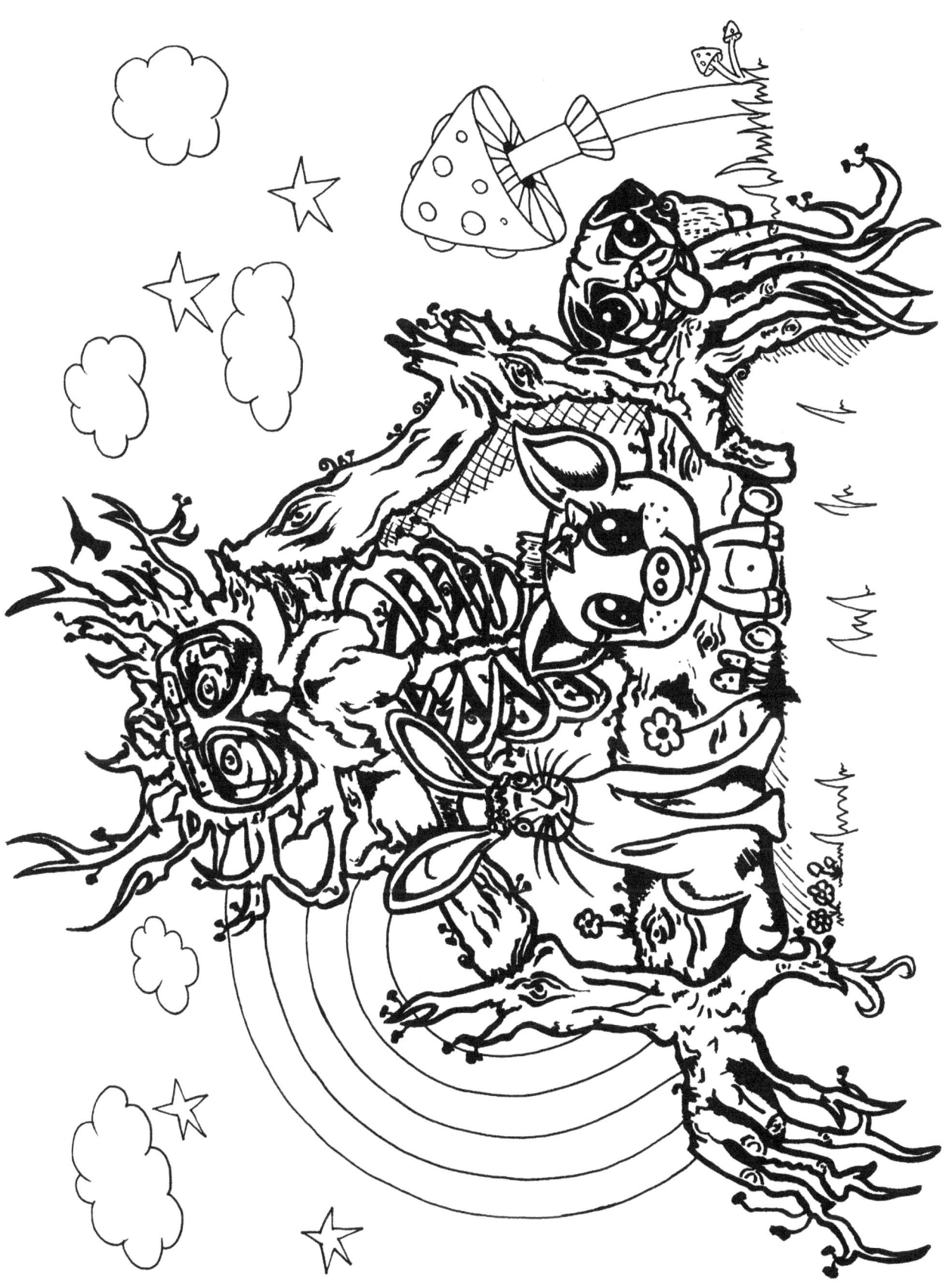

www.ingramcontent.com/pod-product-compliance
Lightning Source LLC
Chambersburg PA
CBHW081909170526

45167CB00007B/3213